test your knowledge of the African continent. Thanks to your knowledge and the geographical indices at the bottom of the page on the map of the continent you will be led to give the capital(s), official languages of the countries.
NB: any country you don't see on the map is most likely on or around the map.


testez vos connaissances du continent africain. Grâce à vos connaissances et aux indices géographiques en bas de page sur la carte du continent vous serez amenez à donnez la/les capitales, langues officielles des pays.

NB: tous pays qui vous paraît absent de la carte est très certainement en bordure ou autour de celle-ci.


the geographical position of each country is marked in white or black on or around the map.

la position géographique de chaque pays est  marquée en  blanc  ou noir sur la carte ou aux alentours .

**Country name** (nom du pays)

............................................

**Country's capital** (Capital)

............................................

## official language(s)
langue(s) officielle(s)

..........................................

## Independence Date
Date de l'indépendance

..........................................

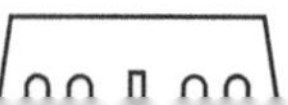

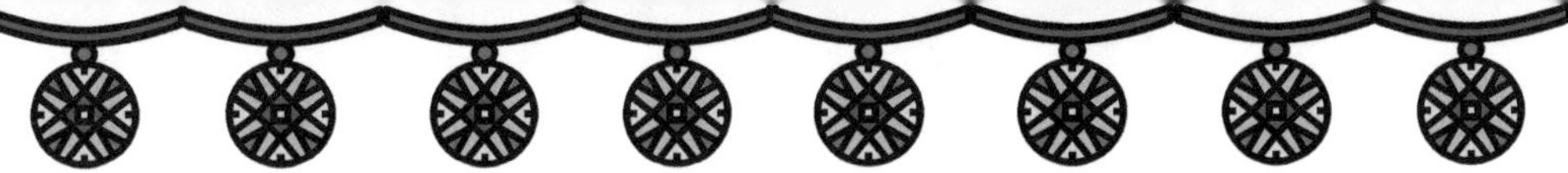

a local saying:
un proverbe local:

*"The Gazelle doesn't drink water when the dog is behind her."*

*"La Gazelle ne boit pas l'eau quand le chien est derrière elle".*

**Country name** (nom du pays) ........................

**Country's capital** (Capital) ........................

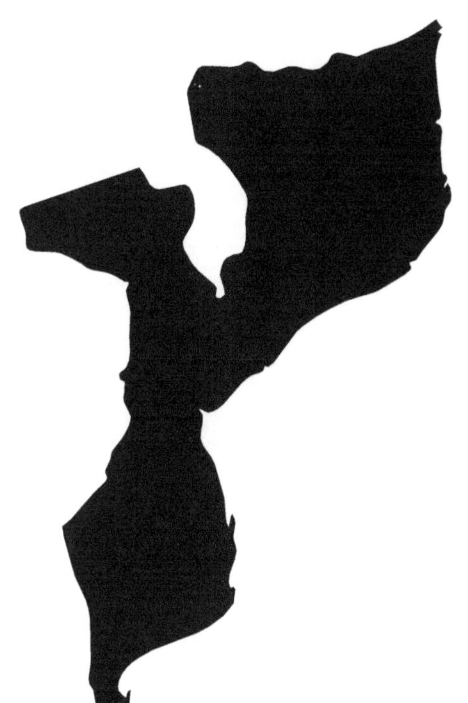

# official language(s)
langue(s) officielle(s)

........................

# Independence Date
Date de l'indépendance

........................

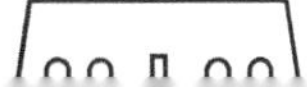

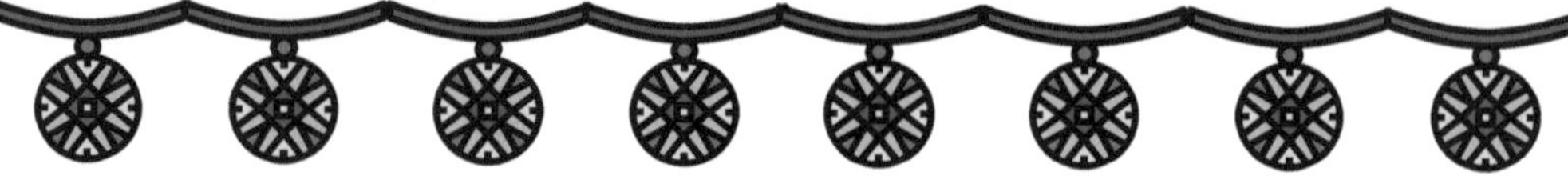

a local saying:

*"Before a bird flies off, I've counted the eggs in its belly."*

un proverbe local:

*"Avant qu'un oiseau ne s'envole, j'ai compté les œufs dans son ventre.".*

**Country name** (nom du pays)  . . . . . . . . . . . . . . . . . . . . . . . .

**Country's capital** (capitale)  . . . . . . . . . . . . . . . . . . . . . . . .

**official language(s)**
langue(s) officielle(s)

. . . . . . . . . . . . . . . . . . . . . . . . . . . . . . . . . . . .

**Independence Date**
Date de l'indépendance

. . . . . . . . . . . . . . . . . . . . . . . . . . . . . . . .

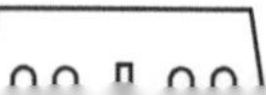

**Country name** (nom du pays)  · · · · · · · · · · · · · · · · · · · ·

**Country's capital** (Capital)  · · · · · · · · · · · · · · · · · · · ·

## official language(s)
langue(s) officielle(s)

· · · · · · · · · · · · · · · · · · · · · · · · · · · · · · · · · · · ·

## Independence Date
Date de l'indépendance

· · · · · · · · · · · · · · · · · · · · · · · · · · · · · · · · · · · ·

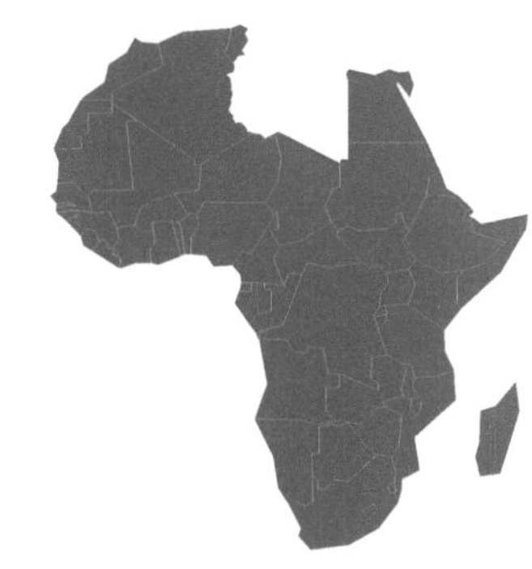

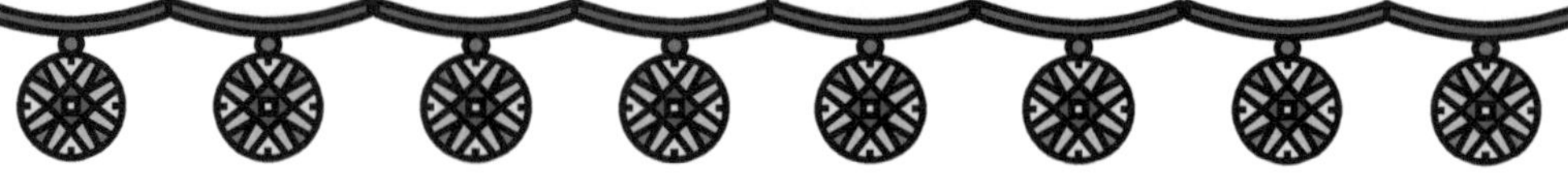



**Country name** _nom du pays_ ● ● ● ● ● ● ● ● ● ● ● ● ● ● ● ● ● ● ●

**Country's capital** _la capitale_ ● ● ● ● ● ● ● ● ● ● ● ● ● ● ● ● ● ● ●

## official language(s)
langue(s) officielle(s)

● ● ● ● ● ● ● ● ● ● ● ● ● ● ● ● ● ● ● ● ● ● ● ● ●

## Independence Date
Date de l'indépendance

● ● ● ● ● ● ● ● ● ● ● ● ● ● ● ● ● ● ● ● ● ● ● ● ●

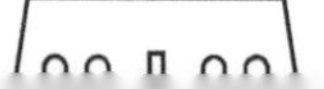

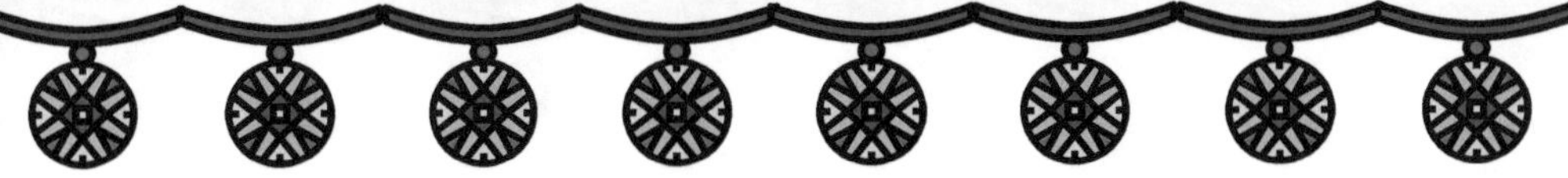



**Country name** (nom du pays) ························

**Country's capital** (Capital) ························

## official language(s)
langue(s) officielle(s)

·····································

## Independence Date
Date de l'indépendance

·····································

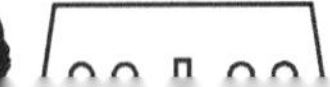

**Country name** (nom du pays) . . . . . . . . . . . . . . . . . . . . . . . .

**Country's capital** (Capital) . . . . . . . . . . . . . . . . . . . . . . . .

# official language(s)
langue(s) officielle(s)

. . . . . . . . . . . . . . . . . . . . . . . . . . . . . . . . . . . . . . . . . . .

# Independence Date
Date de l'indépendance

. . . . . . . . . . . . . . . . . . . . . . . . . . . . . . . . . . . . . . . . . . .

**Country name** (nom du pays) ·····································

**Country's capital** (Capital) ·····································

## official language(s)
langue(s) officielle(s)

·····································

## Independence Date
Date de l'indépendance

·····································

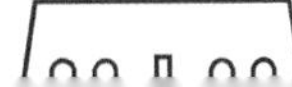

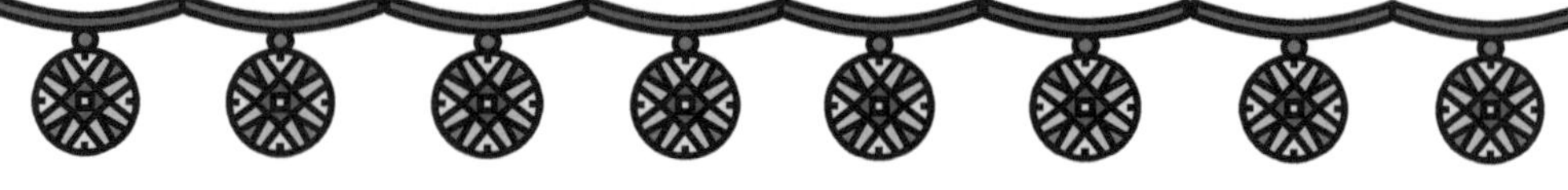



**Country name** (nom du pays)   · · · · · · · · · · · · · · · · · · · · · · · · ·

**Country's capital** (capitale)   · · · · · · · · · · · · · · · · · · · · · · · · ·

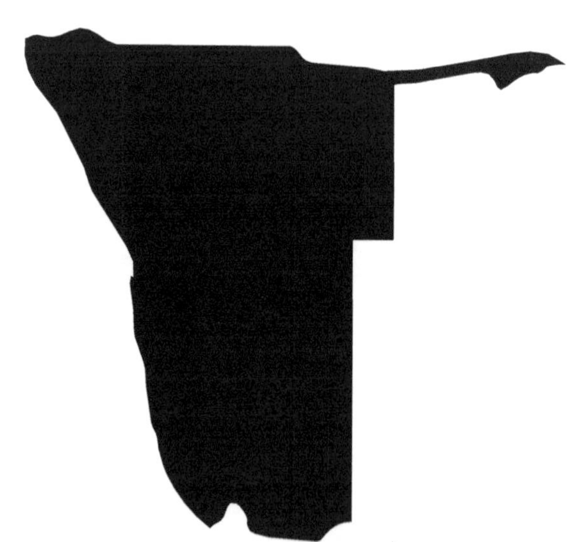

## official language(s)
langue(s) officielle(s)

· · · · · · · · · · · · · · · · · · · · · · · · · · · · · · · ·

## Independence Date
Date de l'indépendance

· · · · · · · · · · · · · · · · · · · · · · · · · · · · · · · ·

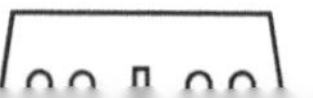

a local saying: *"It's the method that gets the rope to the bottom of the well."*

un proverbe local: *"C'est la méthode qui fait arriver la corde au fond du puits."*

**Country name** (nom du pays) ······························

**Country's capital** (Capital) ······························

# official language(s)
langue(s) officielle(s)

······························

# Independence Date
Date de l'indépendance

······························

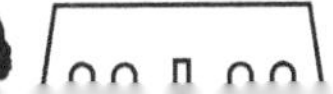

<table>
<tr><td>a local saying:<br>un proverbe local:</td><td>"It's the behavior we follow, because the behavior is the man."<br>"C'est le comportement que l'on suit, car le comportement, c'est l'homme."</td></tr>
</table>

**Country name** nom du pays . . . . . . . . . . . . . . . . . . . . . . . . .

**Country's capital** la capitale . . . . . . . . . . . . . . . . . . . . . . . . .

## official language(s)
langue(s) officielle(s)

. . . . . . . . . . . . . . . . . . . . . . . . . . . . . . .

## Independence Date
Date de l'indépendance

. . . . . . . . . . . . . . . . . . . . . . . . . . . . . . .

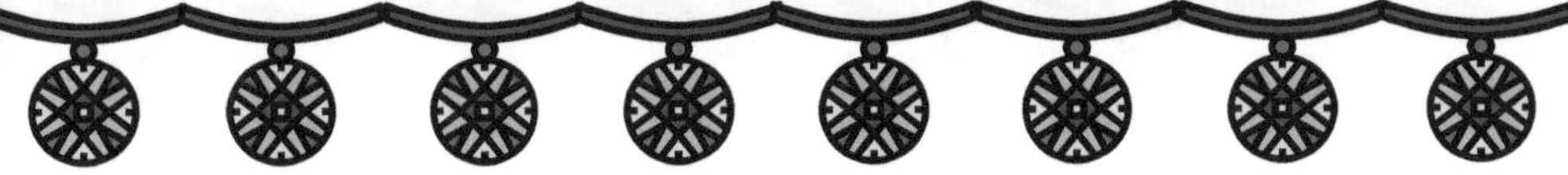



**Country name** (nom du pays)   • • • • • • • • • • • • • • • • • • • •

**Country's capital** (Capital)   • • • • • • • • • • • • • • • • • • •

# official language(s)
langue(s) officielle(s)

• • • • • • • • • • • • • • • • • • • • • • • • • • • •

# Independence Date
Date de l'indépendance

• • • • • • • • • • • • • • • • • • • • • • • • • •

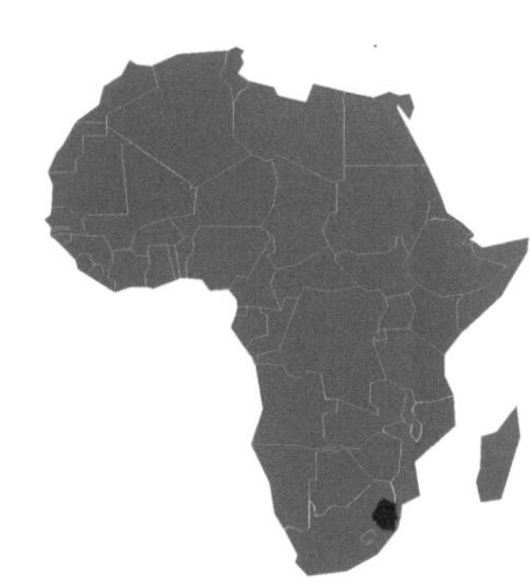

**Country name** (nom du pays)  · · · · · · · · · · · · · · · · · · · · ·

**Country's capital** (Capitale)  · · · · · · · · · · · · · · · · · · · · ·

## official language(s)
langue(s) officielle(s)

· · · · · · · · · · · · · · · · · · · · · · · · · · · · · · · · · · · · ·

## Independence Date
Date de l'indépendance

· · · · · · · · · · · · · · · · · · · · · · · · · · · · · · · · ·

a local saying:     *"When you're a winner, you don't sit on the loser."*
un proverbe local:     *"Lorsque vous êtes vainqueur, vous ne vous asseyez pas sur le vaincu."*

**Country name** (nom du pays) . . . . . . . . . . . . . . . . . . . . .

**Country's capital** (Capital) . . . . . . . . . . . . . . . . . . . . .

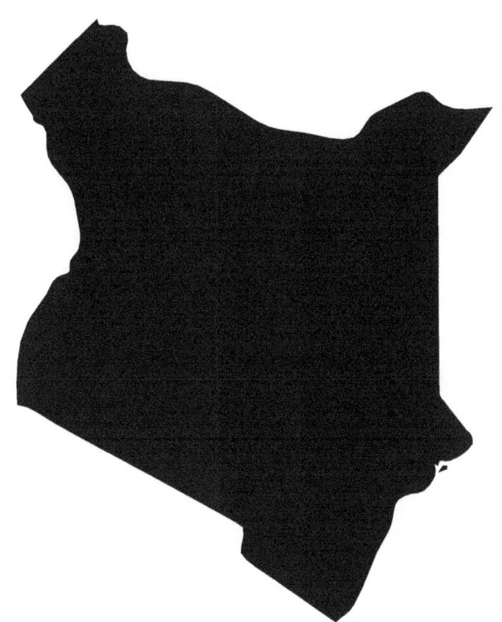

## official language(s)
langue(s) officielle(s)

. . . . . . . . . . . . . . . . . . . . . . . . . . . . . . . . . . . . .

## Independence Date
Date de l'indépendance

. . . . . . . . . . . . . . . . . . . . . . . . . . . . . . . . . . . . .

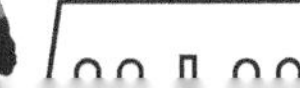

*"Doing it isn't doing it, just kissing your child isn't raising him."*

*"On le fera n'est pas concrétiser, embrasser seulement son enfant n'est pas l'élever."*

**Country name** (nom du pays) • • • • • • • • • • • • • • • • • • • • • •

**Country's capital** (Capital) • • • • • • • • • • • • • • • • • • • • •

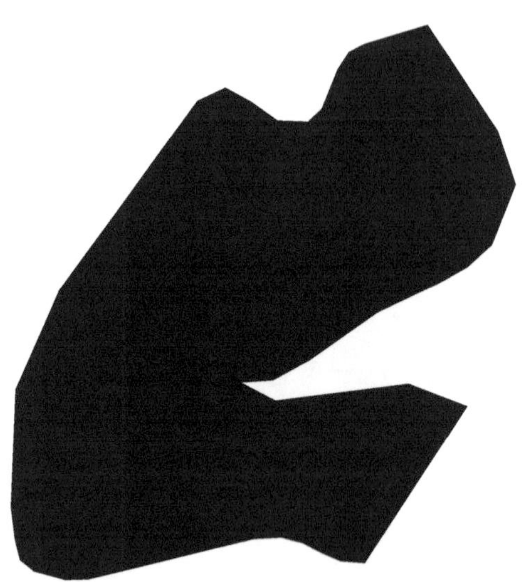

# official language(s)
langue(s) officielle(s)

• • • • • • • • • • • • • • • • • • • • • • • • • • • • • • • •

# Independence Date
Date de l'indépendance

• • • • • • • • • • • • • • • • • • • • • • • • • • • • • • • •

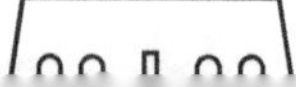

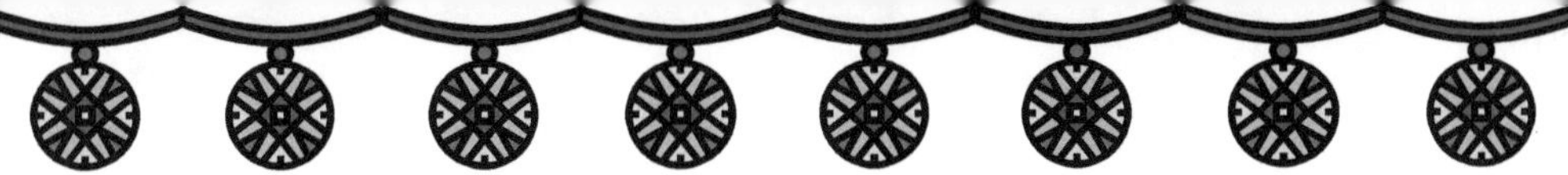

a local saying:  *"When a child isn't hungry, he doesn't know his father's house."*
un proverbe local:  *"Quand un enfant n'a pas faim, il ne connait pas la maison de son père."*

**Country name** (nom du pays)  . . . . . . . . . . . . . . . . . . . . . . .

**Country's capital** (Capital)  . . . . . . . . . . . . . . . . . . . . .

# official language(s)
langue(s) officielle(s)

. . . . . . . . . . . . . . . . . . . . . . . . . . . . . . . . .

# Independence Date
Date de l'indépendance

. . . . . . . . . . . . . . . . . . . . . . . . . . . .

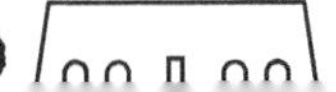

**Country name** *(nom du pays)* • • • • • • • • • • • • • • • • • • • • • •

**Country's capital** *(Capital)* • • • • • • • • • • • • • • • • • • • • • •

## official language(s)
langue(s) officielle(s)

• • • • • • • • • • • • • • • • • • • • • • • • • • • • • • • • • •

## Independence Date
Date de l'indépendance

• • • • • • • • • • • • • • • • • • • • • • • • • • • • • • • • • •

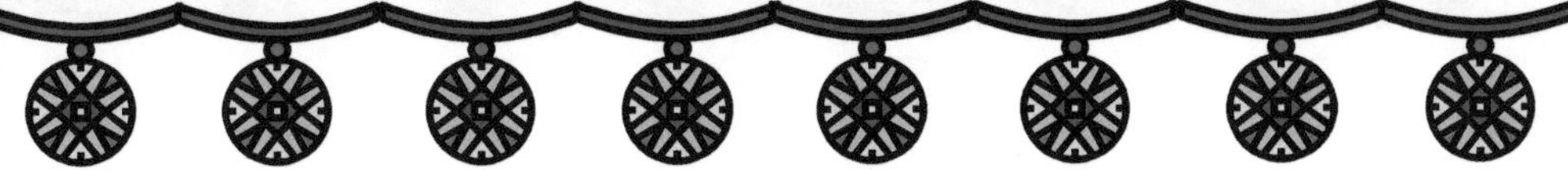

a local saying: *"If you come out of the forest at the same time as the buffalo, know how to climb a tree."*

un proverbe local: *"Si tu sors de la forêt en même temps que le buffle, sache monter à l'arbre."*

## Country name (nom du pays) ..............................

## Country's capital (Capital) ..............................

## official language(s)
langue(s) officielle(s)

...............................................

## Independence Date
Date de l'indépendance

...............................................

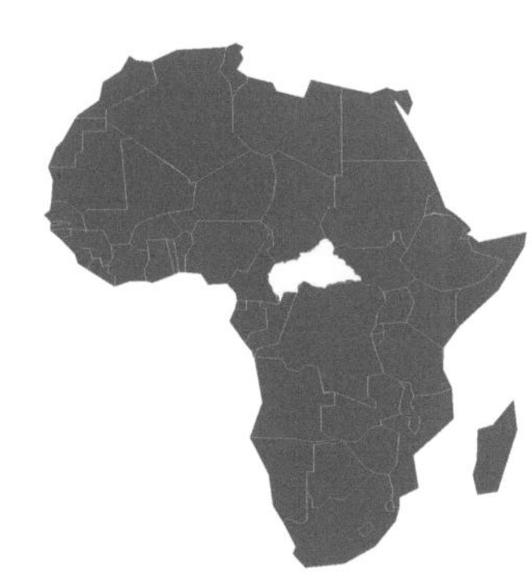

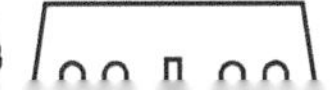

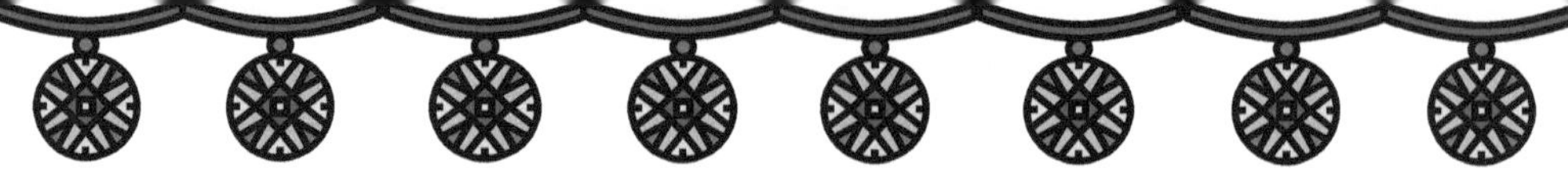



*"Where there is no love, a little nothing becomes a drama. "*

*"Là où il n'y a pas d'amour, un petit rien devient un drame. "*

**Country name** (nom du pays) ● ● ● ● ● ● ● ● ● ● ● ● ● ● ● ● ● ● ● ●

**Country's capital** (Capitale) ● ● ● ● ● ● ● ● ● ● ● ● ● ● ● ● ● ●

## official language(s)
langue(s) officielle(s)

● ● ● ● ● ● ● ● ● ● ● ● ● ● ● ● ● ● ● ● ● ● ● ● ● ● ● ●

## Independence Date
Date de l'indépendance

● ● ● ● ● ● ● ● ● ● ● ● ● ● ● ● ● ● ● ● ● ● ● ● ●

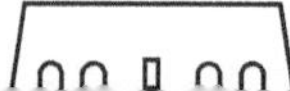

a local saying: *"If you move forward, you die. If you go backwards, you die. Then why move back?"*

un proverbe local: *"Si tu avances, tu meurs. Si tu recules, tu meurs. Alors pourquoi reculer ?"*

**Country name** (nom du pays) ........................................

**Country's capital** (Capital) ........................................

## official language(s)
langue(s) officielle(s)

............................................................

## Independence Date
Date de l'indépendance

............................................................

   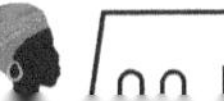      

a local saying:

un proverbe local: *"ne videz pas votre âme à tout le monde et n'y diminuez pas votre importance"*

**Country name** (nom du pays) ............................................

**Country's capital** (Capitale) ............................................

## official language(s)
langue(s) officielle(s)

............................................

## Independence Date
Date de l'indépendance

............................................

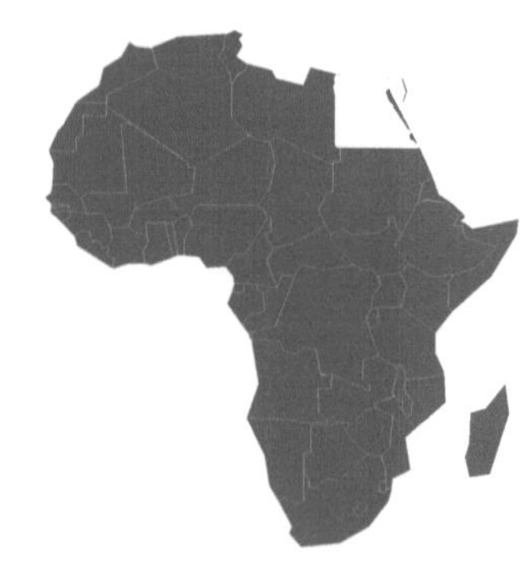

a local saying:

un proverbe local: *"Les hommes peuvent être facilement bons comme ils peuvent être facilement mauvais."*

**Country name** (nom du pays) • • • • • • • • • • • • • • • • • • • • • • •

**Country's capital** (Capital) • • • • • • • • • • • • • • • • • • • • • •

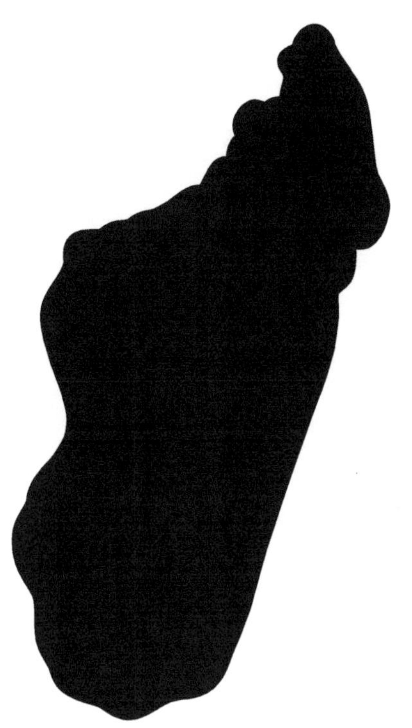

# official language(s)
langue(s) officielle(s)

• • • • • • • • • • • • • • • • • • • • • • • • • • • • • • • • • • • •

# Independence Date
Date de l'indépendance

• • • • • • • • • • • • • • • • • • • • • • • • • • • • • • • • • • • •

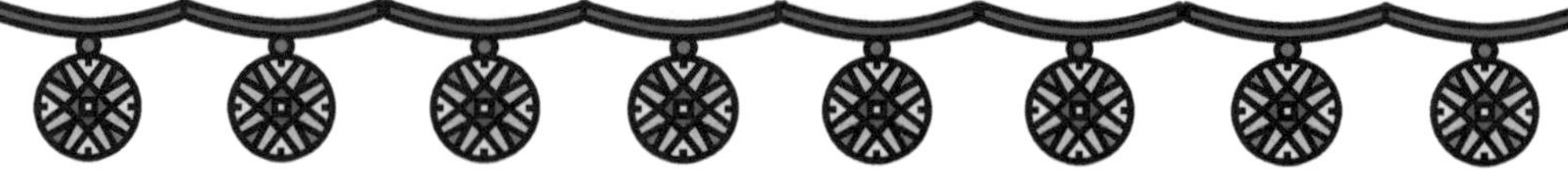



**Country name** nom du pays · · · · · · · · · · · · · · · · · · · ·

**Country's capital** capitale · · · · · · · · · · · · · · · · · · · ·

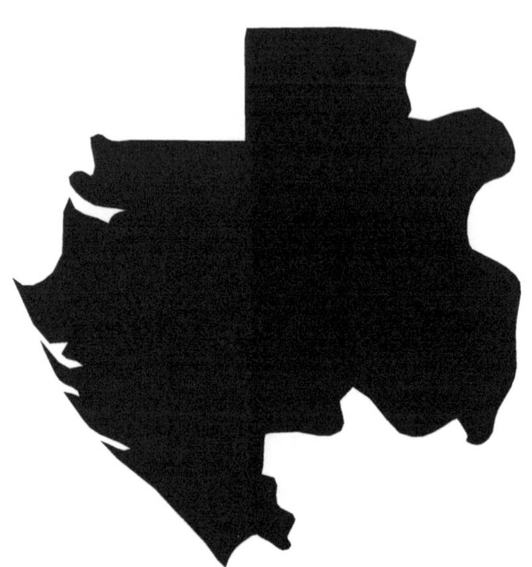

## official language(s)
langue(s) officielle(s)

· · · · · · · · · · · · · · · · · · · · · · · · · · · · · ·

## Independence Date
Date de l'indépendance

· · · · · · · · · · · · · · · · · · · · · · · · · · · ·

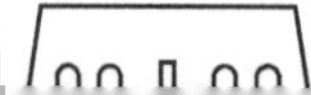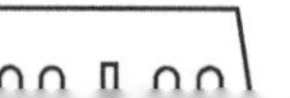

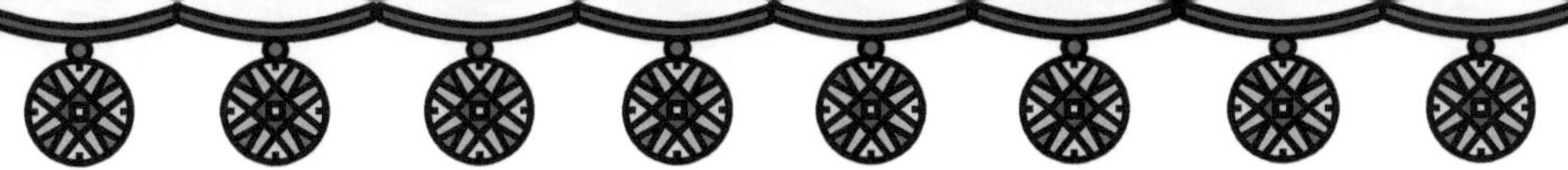

a local saying:
"The path strewn with obstacles is the path to greatness."

un proverbe local:
*"Le chemin parsemé d'obstacles est celui qui mène à la grandeur."*

**Country name** (nom du pays) • • • • • • • • • • • • • • • • • • • • • •

**Country's capital** (Capital) • • • • • • • • • • • • • • • • • • • • • •

# official language(s)
langue(s) officielle(s)

• • • • • • • • • • • • • • • • • • • • • • • • • • • • • • •

# Independence Date
Date de l'indépendance

• • • • • • • • • • • • • • • • • • • • • • • • • • • • • • •

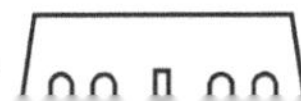

**Country name** nom du pays

**Country's capital** Capitale

## official language(s)
langue(s) officielle(s)

## Independence Date
Date de l'indépendance

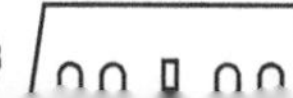

a local saying:  *"You mustn't waste your life earning it."*
un proverbe local:  *"Il ne faut pas perdre sa vie à la gagner."*

**Country name** (nom du pays)  · · · · · · · · · · · · · · · · · · · · · · ·

**Country's capital** (Capital)  · · · · · · · · · · · · · · · · · · · · · · ·

## official language(s)
langue(s) officielle(s)

· · · · · · · · · · · · · · · · · · · · · · · · · · · · · · · · · · ·

## Independence Date
Date de l'indépendance

· · · · · · · · · · · · · · · · · · · · · · · · · · · · · · · · · · ·

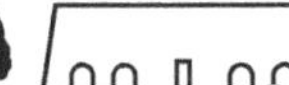

**Country name** (nom du pays) · · · · · · · · · · · · · · · · · · ·

**Country's capital** (capitale) · · · · · · · · · · · · · · · · · · ·

## official language(s)
langue(s) officielle(s)

· · · · · · · · · · · · · · · · · · · · · · · · · · · · ·

## Independence Date
Date de l'indépendance

· · · · · · · · · · · · · · · · · · · · · · · · · · · · ·

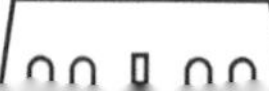

a local saying: *"The mother accepts her child in any situation."*
un proverbe local: *"La mère accepte son enfant quel qu'il soit et dans n'importe quelle situation."*

**Country name** (nom du pays)  · · · · · · · · · · · · · · · · · · · · ·

**Country's capital** (Capital)  · · · · · · · · · · · · · · · · · · · ·

## official language(s)
langue(s) officielle(s)

· · · · · · · · · · · · · · · · · · · · · · · · · · · · · ·

## Independence Date
Date de l'indépendance

· · · · · · · · · · · · · · · · · · · · · · · · · · · · · ·

   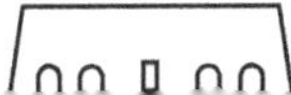     

a local saying:   *"Only your real friends will tell you when your face is dirty."*

un proverbe local:   *"Il n'y a que vos vrais amis qui vous diront quand votre face est sale"*

**Country name** (nom du pays) · · · · · · · · · · · · · · · · · · · · · ·

**Country's capital** (capitale) · · · · · · · · · · · · · · · · · · · · · ·

## official language(s)
langue(s) officielle(s)

· · · · · · · · · · · · · · · · · · · · · · · · · · · · · · · · ·

## Independence Date
Date de l'indépendance

· · · · · · · · · · · · · · · · · · · · · · · · · · · · · · · · ·

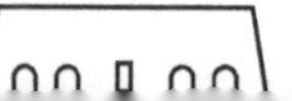

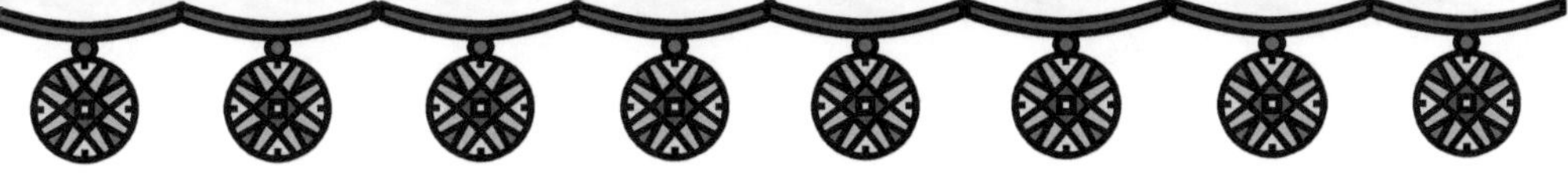



**Country name** (nom du pays)  · · · · · · · · · · · · · · · · · ·

**Country's capital** (Capital)  · · · · · · · · · · · · · · · · · ·

# official language(s)
langue(s) officielle(s)

· · · · · · · · · · · · · · · · · · · · · · · · · · · · · · · · · · · ·

# Independence Date
Date de l'indépendance

· · · · · · · · · · · · · · · · · · · · · · · · · · ·

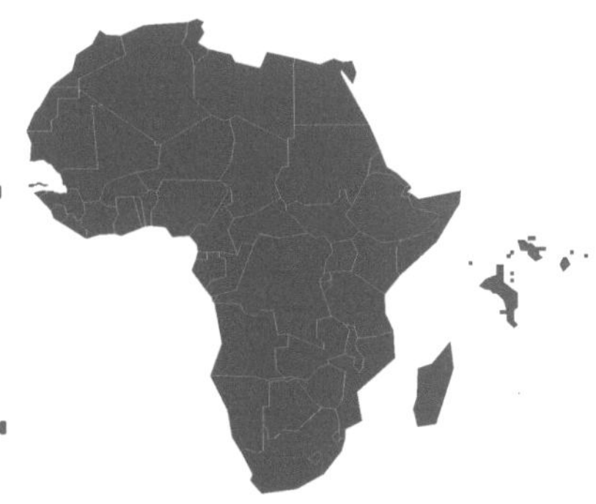

*"The teeth may laugh, but the heart knows the wound it bears."*

*"Les dents ont beau rire, le cœur sait la blessure qu'il porte."*

**Country name** (nom du pays) . . . . . . . . . . . . . . . . . . . . . . . . .

**Country's capital** (Capitale) . . . . . . . . . . . . . . . . . . . . . . . . .

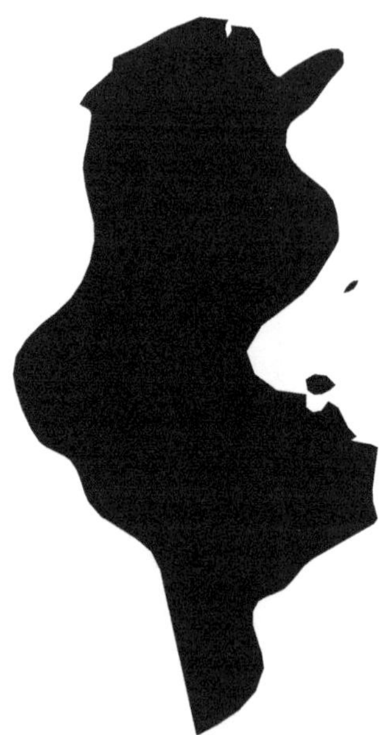

## official language(s)
langue(s) officielle(s)

. . . . . . . . . . . . . . . . . . . . . . . . . . . . . . . . . . . . . . . . . .

## Independence Date
Date de l'indépendance

. . . . . . . . . . . . . . . . . . . . . . . . . . . . . . . . . . . . . . . . . .

a local saying:     *"only those who live together quarrel."*
un proverbe local:     *"seuls ceux qui vivent ensemble se disputent."*

**Country name** (nom du pays)     · · · · · · · · · · · · · · · · · · · · · · · · · ·

**Country's capital** (Capital)     · · · · · · · · · · · · · · · · · · · · · · · · · ·

## official language(s)
langue(s) officielle(s)

· · · · · · · · · · · · · · · · · · · · · · · · · · · · · · · · · · · · ·

## Independence Date
Date de l'indépendance

· · · · · · · · · · · · · · · · · · · · · · · · · · · · · · · · · · · · ·

a local saying: *"It's together that the monkeys gather the fruit."*

un proverbe local: *"C'est ensemble que les singes ramassent les fruits."*

**Country name** · · · · · · · · · · · · · · · · · · · ·

**Country's capital** · · · · · · · · · · · · · · · · · · · ·

## official language(s)
langue(s) officielle(s)

· · · · · · · · · · · · · · · · · · · · · · · ·

## Independence Date
Date de l'indépendance

· · · · · · · · · · · · · · · · · · · · · · · ·

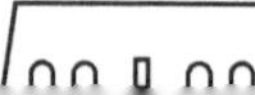

a local saying:
un proverbe local:

*"Whoever teases a wasp's nest must know how to run."*

*"Quiconque taquine un nid de guêpes doit savoir courir."*

**Country name** (nom du pays)  · · · · · · · · · · · · · · · · · · · · · · · ·

**Country's capital** (Capital)  · · · · · · · · · · · · · · · · · · · · · ·

# official language(s)
langue(s) officielle(s)

· · · · · · · · · · · · · · · · · · · · · · · · · · · · · · · · · · · · · · ·

# Independence Date
Date de l'indépendance

· · · · · · · · · · · · · · · · · · · · · · · · · · · · · · · · · · · · · · ·

a local saying: *"Listen to what they say about your friend; listen for yourself, too."*

un proverbe local: *"Écoute ce qu'on dit de ton ami; écoute pour toi également."*

**Country name** · · · · · · · · · · · · · · · · · · · · · · · ·

**Country's capital** · · · · · · · · · · · · · · · · · · · · · · · ·

## official language(s)
langue(s) officielle(s)

· · · · · · · · · · · · · · · · · · · · · · · · · · · · · · · ·

## Independence Date
Date de l'indépendance

· · · · · · · · · · · · · · · · · · · · · · · · · · · · · · · ·

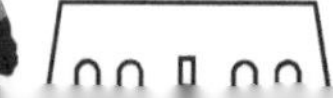

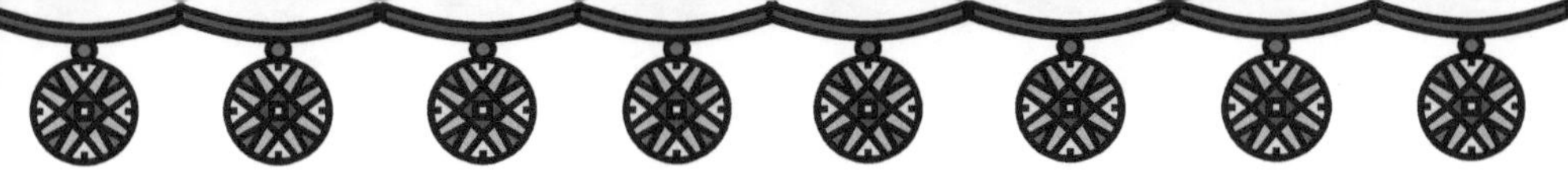

a local saying:  *"Mercy for a child comes from its mother."*
un proverbe local:  *" La pitié pour un enfant vient de sa mère."*

**Country name** (nom du pays)  · · · · · · · · · · · · · · · · · · · · · ·

**Country's capital** (Capital)  · · · · · · · · · · · · · · · · · · · · · ·

## official language(s)
langue(s) officielle(s)

· · · · · · · · · · · · · · · · · · · · · · · · · · · · · · · ·

## Independence Date
Date de l'indépendance

· · · · · · · · · · · · · · · · · · · · · · · · · · · · · · · ·

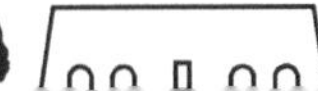

a local saying:  *"Teeth are all friends with each other."*
un proverbe local: *" Les dents sont toutes amies entre elles."*

**Country name**

**Country's capital**

**official language(s)**
langue(s) officielle(s)

**Independence Date**
Date de l'indépendance

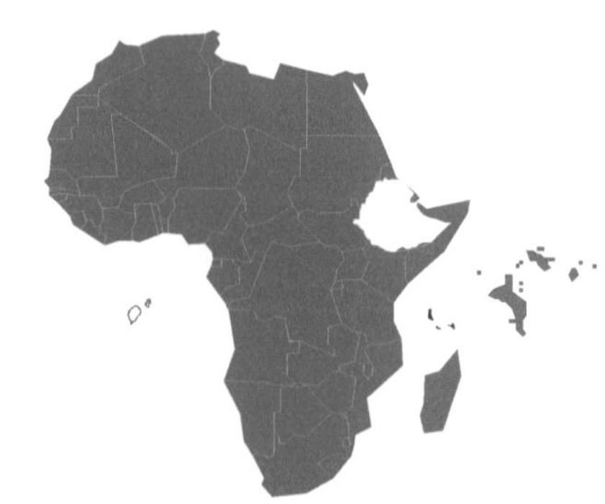

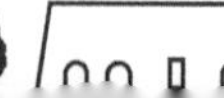

**Country name** (nom du pays) . . . . . . . . . . . . . . . . . . . . . . . . . . . .

**Country's capital** (Capitale) . . . . . . . . . . . . . . . . . . . . . . . . . . . .

## official language(s)
langue(s) officielle(s)

. . . . . . . . . . . . . . . . . . . . . . . . . . . . . . . . . . . . . . . . .

## Independence Date
Date de l'indépendance

. . . . . . . . . . . . . . . . . . . . . . . . . . . . . . . . . . . . . . . . .

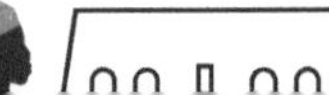

a local saying: *"The rich is an example to the poor and the poor is a warning to the rich."*

un proverbe local: *"Le riche est un exemple pour le pauvre et le pauvre est un avertissement pour le riche."*

**Country name** . . . . . . . . . . . . . . . . . . . . .

**Country's capital** . . . . . . . . . . . . . . . . . . . . .

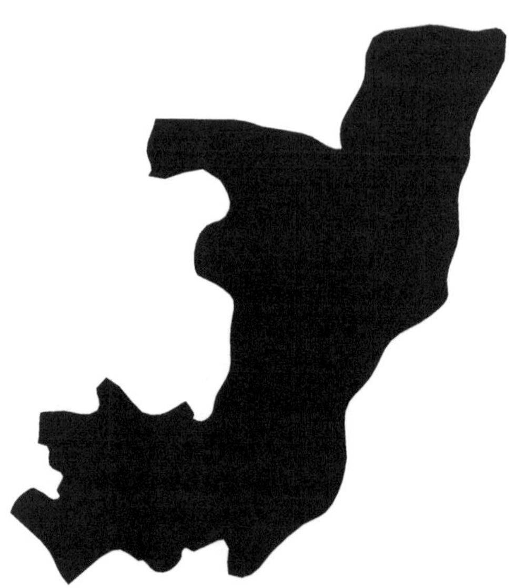

## official language(s)
langue(s) officielle(s)

. . . . . . . . . . . . . . . . . . . . . . . . . . . . . .

## Independence Date
Date de l'indépendance

. . . . . . . . . . . . . . . . . . . . . . . . . . . . . .

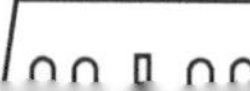

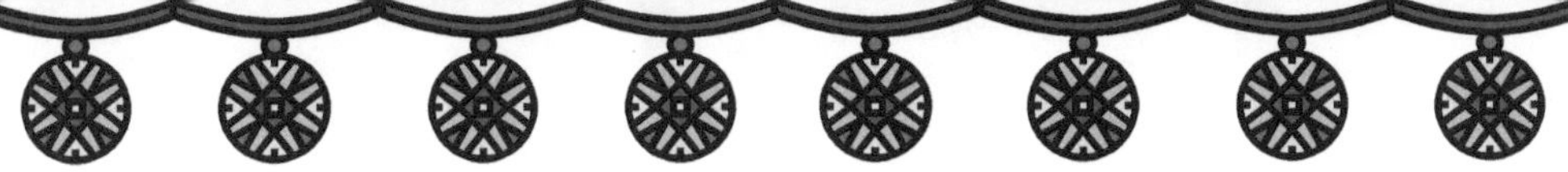

a local saying: *"If things change, it's because people talk about it. If they don't, they'll go on like that forever."*

un proverbe local: *"Si les choses changent, c'est parce que les gens en parlent.Sinon, elles continueraient ainsi éternellement."*

**Country name** (nom du pays) · · · · · · · · · · · · · · · · · · ·

**Country's capital** (Capitale) · · · · · · · · · · · · · · · · · · ·

## official language(s)
langue(s) officielle(s)

· · · · · · · · · · · · · · · · · · · · · · · · ·

## Independence Date
Date de l'indépendance

· · · · · · · · · · · · · · · · · · · · · · · · ·

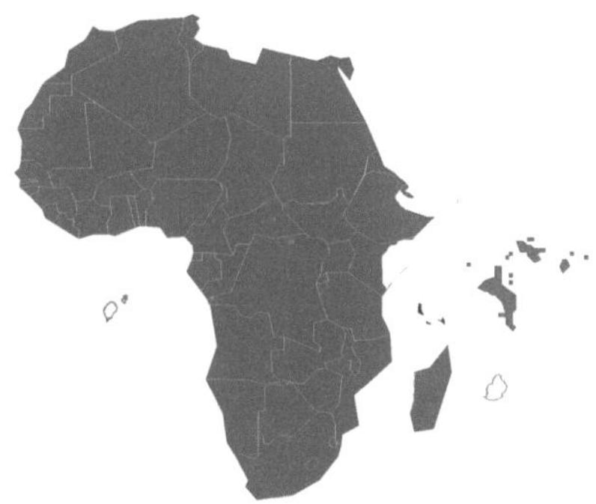

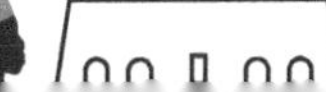

**Country name**

**Country's capital**

## official language(s)
langue(s) officielle(s)

## Independence Date
Date de l'indépendance

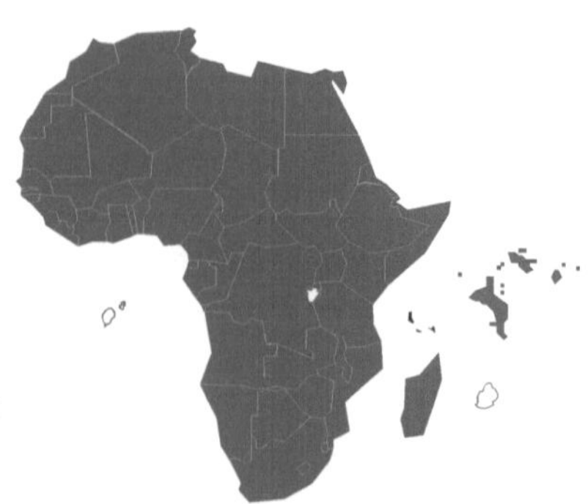

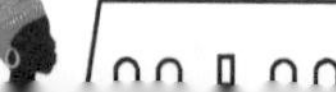

a local saying: *"the tears that run down your face won't stop you from seeing."*

un proverbe local: *"Les pleurs qui coulent sur votre visage ne vous empêcheront pas de voir."*

**Country name** (nom du pays) • • • • • • • • • • • • • • • • • • • • • •

**Country's capital** (Capital) • • • • • • • • • • • • • • • • • • • • •

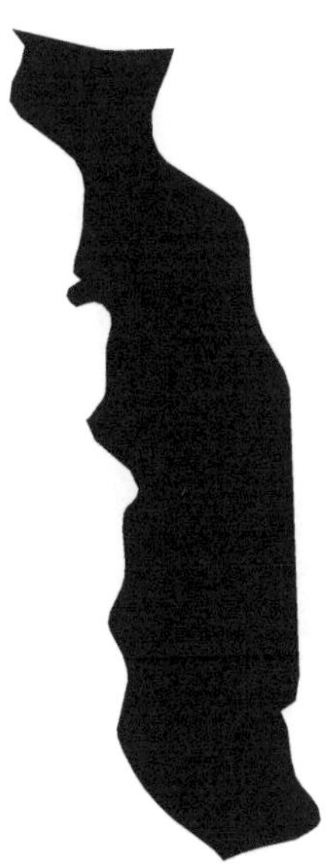

## official language(s)
langue(s) officielle(s)

• • • • • • • • • • • • • • • • • • • • • • • • • • • •

## Independence Date
Date de l'indépendance

• • • • • • • • • • • • • • • • • • • • • •

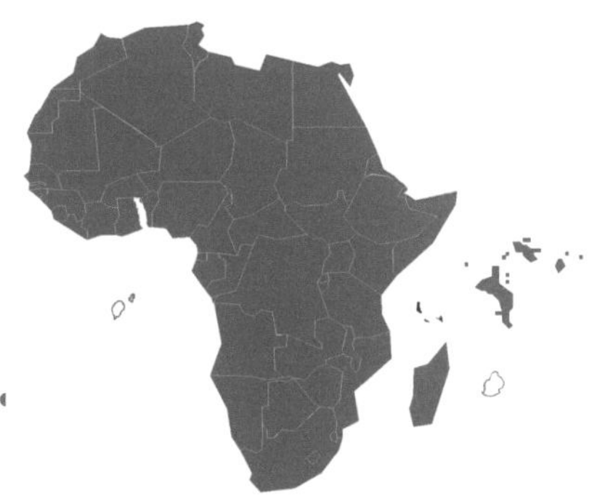

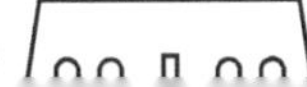

a local saying:     *"The stranger has big eyes but can't see."*
un proverbe local:*"L'étranger a de gros yeux mais ne voit pas"*

**Country name**

**Country's capital**

**official language(s)**
langue(s) officielle(s)

**Independence Date**
Date de l'indépendance

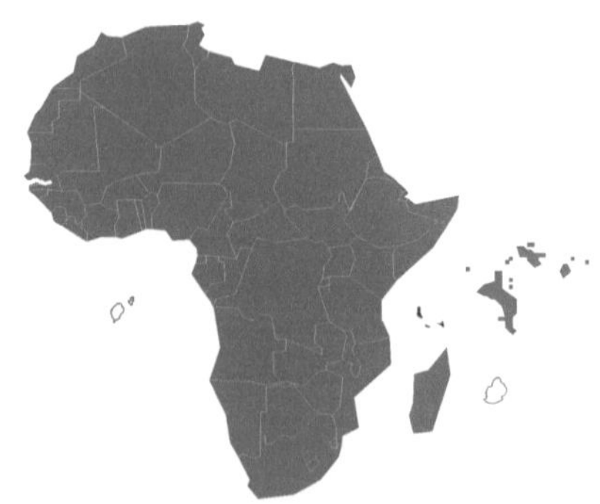

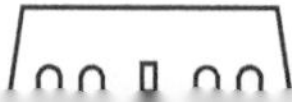

**Country name** (nom du pays) ● ● ● ● ● ● ● ● ● ● ● ● ● ● ● ● ●

**Country's capital** (Capital) ● ● ● ● ● ● ● ● ● ● ● ● ● ● ● ● ●

# official language(s)
langue(s) officielle(s)

● ● ● ● ● ● ● ● ● ● ● ● ● ● ● ● ● ● ● ● ● ● ● ●

# Independence Date
Date de l'indépendance

● ● ● ● ● ● ● ● ● ● ● ● ● ● ● ● ● ● ● ● ● ● ●

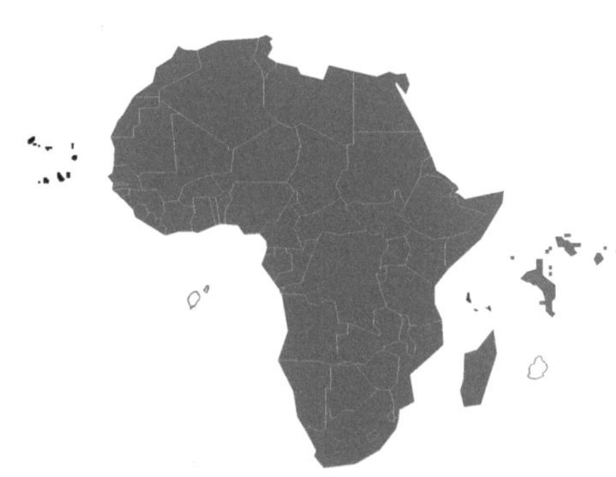

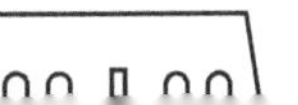

a local saying:

un proverbe local:

**Country name** ........................................

**Country's capital** ........................................

## official language(s)
langue(s) officielle(s)

........................................

## Independence Date
Date de l'indépendance

........................................

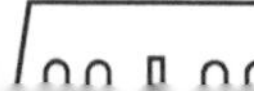

a local saying:  *"A leader is a leader by the grace of the people."*
un proverbe local:    *" un chef est chef par la grâce du peuple "*

**Country name** (nom du pays)  · · · · · · · · · · · · · · · · · ·

**Country's capital** (Capital)  · · · · · · · · · · · · · · · · · ·

## official language(s)
langue(s) officielle(s)

· · · · · · · · · · · · · · · · · · · · · · · · ·

## Independence Date
Date de l'indépendance

· · · · · · · · · · · · · · · · · · · ·

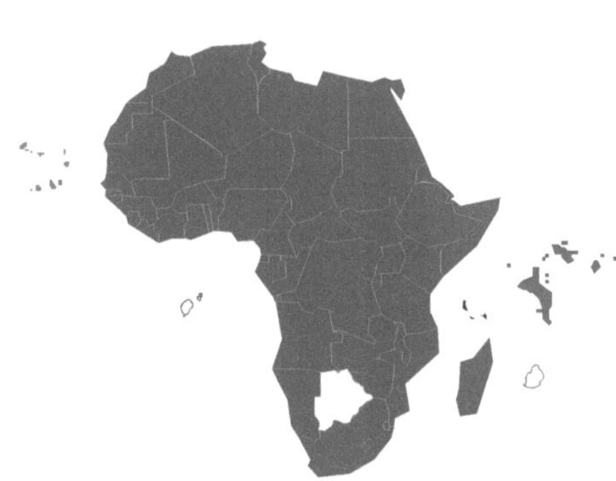

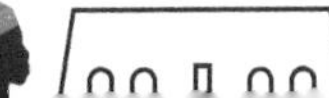

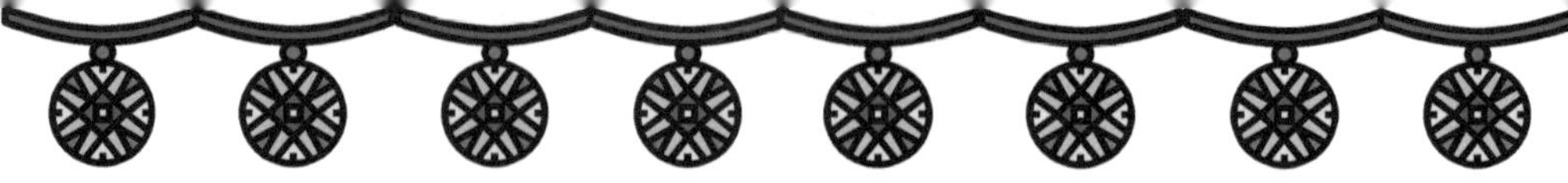

a local saying: *"Squatting in front of the dwarf won't keep you from regaining your original height."*

un proverbe local: *"t'accroupir devant le nain ne t'empêchera pas de retrouver ta taille initiale."*

**Country name** (nom du pays) . . . . . . . . . . . . . . . . . . . . . . . . .

**Country's capital** (Capital) . . . . . . . . . . . . . . . . . . . . . . . . .

## official language(s)
langue(s) officielle(s)

. . . . . . . . . . . . . . . . . . . . . . . . . . . . . . . . .

## Independence Date
Date de l'indépendance

. . . . . . . . . . . . . . . . . . . . . . . . . .

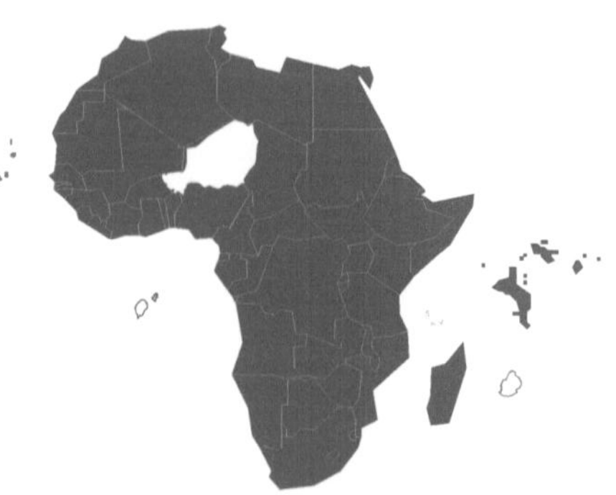

a local saying:
un proverbe local:

"We prefer poverty in freedom to opulence in slavery."
*"Nous préférons la pauvreté dans la liberté à l'opulence dans l'esclavage."*

**Country name** (nom du pays) ·····················

**Country's capital** (Capital) ·····················

## official language(s)
langue(s) officielle(s)

·····················

## Independence Date
Date de l'indépendance

·····················

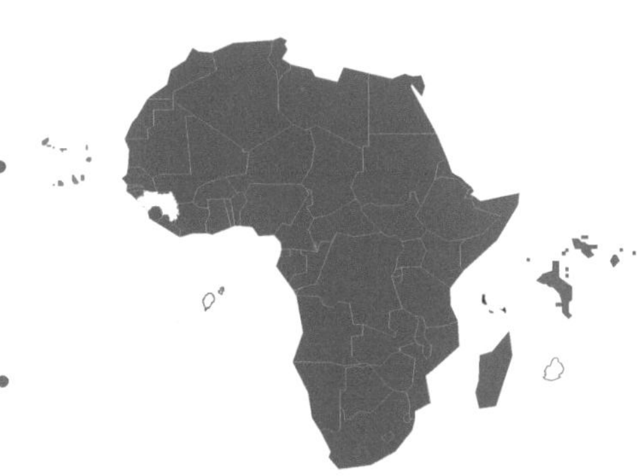

   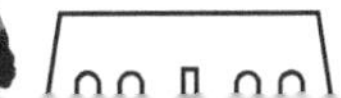      

**Country name** · · · · · · · · · · · · · · · · · · · ·

**Country's capital** · · · · · · · · · · · · · · · · · ·

## official language(s)
langue(s) officielle(s)

· · · · · · · · · · · · · · · · · · · · · · · · · ·

## Independence Date
Date de l'indépendance

· · · · · · · · · · · · · · · · · · · · · · · · ·

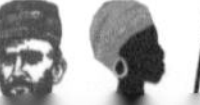

**Country name** (nom du pays) · · · · · · · · · · · · · · · · · · · ·

**Country's capital** (Capital) · · · · · · · · · · · · · · · · · ·

## official language(s)
langue(s) officielle(s)

· · · · · · · · · · · · · · · · · · · · · · · ·

## Independence Date
Date de l'indépendance

· · · · · · · · · · · · · · · · · · · · · · · ·

a local saying:     *"The man in a hurry won't get very far..."*
un proverbe local:     *"L'homme pressé n'ira pas très loin..."*

**Country name**

**Country's capital**

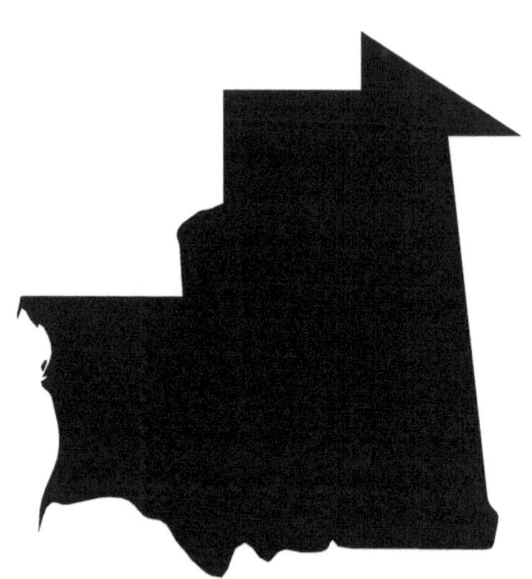

## official language(s)
langue(s) officielle(s)

## Independence Date
Date de l'indépendance

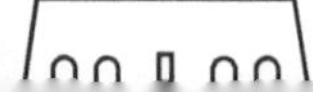

a local saying:

*"Death is in the folds of our mantle. Death can be found anywhere, anytime."*

un proverbe local:

*"La mort est dans les plis de notre manteau : on peut trouver la mort n'importe où et n'importe quand."*

**Country name** (nom du pays)  · · · · · · · · · · · · · · · · · · · ·

**Country's capital** (Capital)  · · · · · · · · · · · · · · · · · · · ·

# official language(s)
langue(s) officielle(s)

· · · · · · · · · · · · · · · · · · · · · · · · · ·

# Independence Date
Date de l'indépendance

· · · · · · · · · · · · · · · · · · · · · · · ·

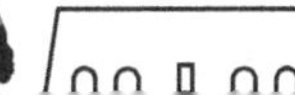

a local saying: *"The monkey doesn't say his son is ugly."*
un proverbe local: *"Le singe ne dit pas que son fils est laid."*

**Country name**

**Country's capital**

**official language(s)**
langue(s) officielle(s)

**Independence Date**
Date de l'indépendance

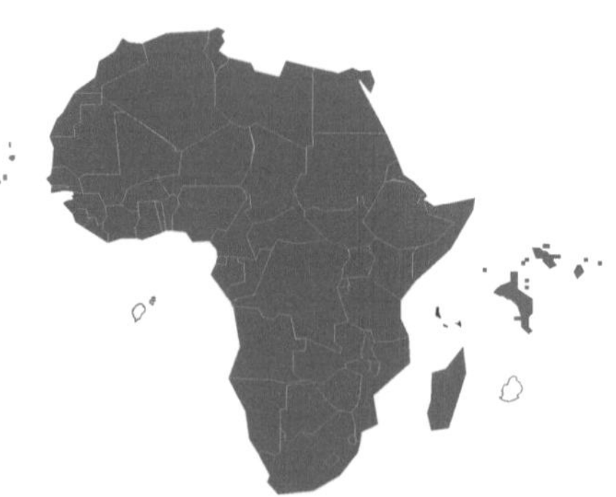

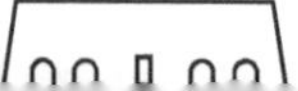

> *"Nonsense, the girl who teaches her mother how to give birth."*



> *"Insensée la fille qui apprend à sa mère à enfanter."*

**Country name** (nom du pays)  · · · · · · · · · · · · · · · · · · · ·

**Country's capital** (Capital)  · · · · · · · · · · · · · · · · · · ·

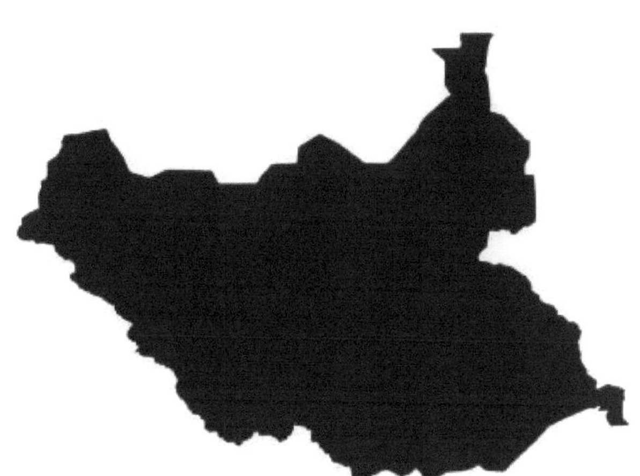

## official language(s)
langue(s) officielle(s)

· · · · · · · · · · · · · · · · · · · ·

## Independence Date
Date de l'indépendance

· · · · · · · · · · · · · · · · · · · ·

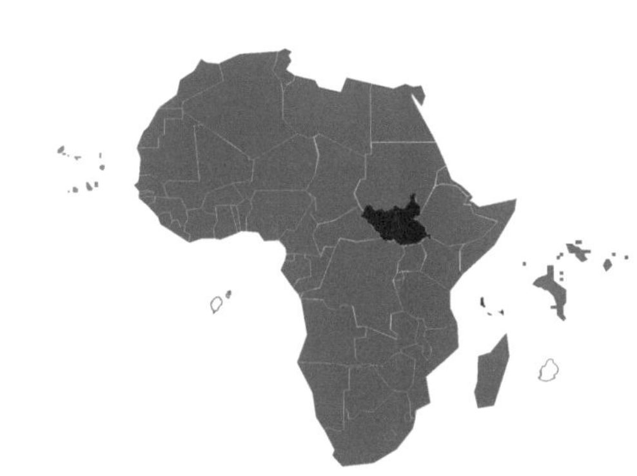

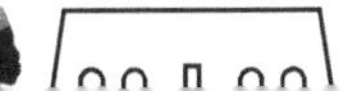

"Le bonheur ne s'acquiert pas, il ne réside pas dans les apparences, chacun d'entre nous le construit à chaque instant de sa vie avec son coeur"



"Happiness is not acquired, it does not reside in appearances, each one of us builds it in every moment of our life with our heart."